Hello, World!

Jory Wernette

BookLeaf
Publishing

Presentation by *BookLeaf Publishing*

Web: www.bookleafpub.com

E-mail: info@bookleafpub.com

ISBN: 9789357210904

First edition 2022

DEDICATION

I want to thank my family and friends- thank you for supporting me doing whatever I feel like whenever I feel like and still continuing to be there for me.

Thank you, Mom, Dad, Jess, Bill, my grandparents, Moke, Casey, Kyleigh, Kloe and my friends, Nick, Jack, Michael, Sam, another Sam, Aaron, Ramiro, and Jessie. I would make this list longer, but I am going to go roller skating. Know that I love you all very much, no matter how sassy I am with all of you.

ACKNOWLEDGEMENT

I want to give a thank you to my professors Jim Glasgow and Bob Trapp. Thank you for putting up with me in class and teaching me your ways. I hope I do not disappoint.

PREFACE

I recently watched one of my favorite movies, "Yes Man" starring Jim Carrey. That movie is the cause of this little project and other such situations I have found myself in lately, like being one of the three bachelors on a Live Dating Game show and accidentally joining a Roller Derby team.

I am a Professional

It took all week to fix all this code
To stop the trend - it likes to explode
It's time to leave soon
It's Friday past noon
I'm a buffoon - it's time upload

404

Evaluating my mistakes from yesterday
Rereading impossible scribbles
Resolving this issue will take way longer than it
should
Overwhelming imposter syndrome
Really, whoever hired me should be fired

Constantly hitting ctrl+z or ctrl+c/v
Overcoming these mistakes
Developer life is a cycle of two steps forward
one step back
Even still I get another error

var i;

In code we work with data types
We will store this info in bytes
We know which kind will work just right

In life we search for who we are
Some aim to be a superstar
For now I'll just declare I'm var

The View from my Window

The view from my window is beautiful.
It shows me a scene that I exalt.
Many people have seem the view from my
window and thought nothing of it.
It is like the sky on the way to a mountain's
summit-
Something everyone sees, but is not the focus of
their salt.

The view from my window is meaningful.
It would mean more to people if they'd take a
moment to halt.
If they would pay attention to more than just the
mountain and look above it.
They might just find they would come to love it.
I know I could change the view from my
window- its just the default.

Flow

5

They say you are in flow when you are focused
on what you are doing.
Time passes and you do not notice.

Flow comes to me when I code.
For others, it may be music, like playing harp,
but for me it is whenever I use C#

Everything in its Right Place

In code there are certain practices (C#
myFavorite)
Bracket here
   Indent to do the work. Semicolon.
     If needed,
       Another bracket.
         Indent further to do more work.
Semicolon.
       Another bracket.
     For every time your code gets more
complicated,
       Another bracket.
         Indent further. Semicolon.
       Another bracket.
     Return only what you intend to continue
using, C# myFavorite
Finally, the last bracket here

A Day in the Life

I roll out of bed
An hour after my alarm was set-
This is still an hour before my boss will even
consider setting his alarm.
I am a programmer.

Another great day of being like a fan
blowing into the sails of a mighty ship,
but I am sitting on its deck.
I am an expert.

Another productive day problem solving
how to move soup from one bowl to the next,
but I am given two forks.
I am a professional.

Another day scribbling nonsense
mostly with only the keys of a keyboard
that no one likes to press
I am a programmer.

Nothing Like It

When people give examples of the greatest thing
in the world,
they might say
   a child's laughter
   free food
   and love at first sight.

What they do not know is that there is more:
   spending an entire day
   not debugging once
   and yet your solution builds in your very first
try.

The Daily Loop

```
Foreach(moment in everyDay)
{
  try
  {
    makeTheMost();
    appreciate();
    learn();
  }
  catch(Exception iTried)
  {
    return iTried;
  }
}
```

A Big Problem

I heard once from a Ted Talk
that there is no such thing as a big problem,
only little problems strung together.

Honestly, this helped my focus one new projects
without making me balk.
Just take the lot of my data and focus on my
intended column.
This makes the workload ad light as a feather.

What I Do

My family asks me what I even do.
I tell them I am not even sure.
But they know I work with computers.
And they know I do not have to be a commuter.
They know I am not a doctor looking for some
cure.

My family may not know what I do.
They may not really even care.
But they know, when it comes to computers, I
am always prepared.

Alphabet Remix

All of coding is kind of remixing the alphabet:
literature jazz.
Brainstorming solutions and fixes to a query are
what make me very happy.

I may not need the full alphabet,
but It is fun to know it is there if I need it.

Bad Days

Some days on the job are not very good:
I cannot fix an issue,
I cannot get past an error screen,
or I cannot even center my div.

Some days feel like I am the dumbest one on the
planet:
even though this may not always be true,
for a while it certainly feels like it.

Some days I am racking my brain for an answer
that just will not come.
But its fun to realize that these days happen-
And they are the reason that coders can have
good days.

Being a Coder

When I talk about being a coder,
people may think I am just a code monkey
and I do nothing but type.
Let me tell you, there is more to the hype.
That everything can change with the use of one
key.

We are not that guy from the movie- the nerd
with the odor.
We do usually make a little more money
and we are a little bit smarter than your average
tyke.
We work in the real world but most of us would
prefer the fey.

Applications

Coding has many applications.
Professionally, I am a web developer.
This means I work on websites.
I am what makes that youtube play button play.
What makes the Google Search button search.

But coding has other applications.
In the past, I learned to code to figure out
complex math problems.
I learned the fundamentals of coding
while solving my college level maths.

And yet, coding has more applications.
In the future, I would like to be a video game
developer.
To be the reason a Pokeball can catch a pocket
monster.
To be the reason you can climb mountains and
clip through walls

Even still, coding has more applications.
Like those Icons on everyone's phones.
There is always another application.

Sources

Whenever a problem arises
There are certain sources that we all flock to
W3Schools,
Stackoverflow,
or the Developer Documentations,
or even a coworker who has been on job longer.

Each has its own attitude and use for each
problem.
W3schools for when I need the most basic of
information.
Stackoverflow for when copy pasting is the way
to go.
Documentations for when I am doing something
more complex.
And a coworker for when I feel like hearing
some sass and an answer.

What makes me a good programmer is not that I
know everything,
but I know when there is an issue, that I can find
a source

IT

While I was hired on to be a Web Developer,
my role has expanded to be that of IT.
I may fix issues and answer emails,
I never answer the phone.

I may be the one to make your computer work,
but the secret is to turn it off and back on.

If that does not work we are downloading adobe
reader again.

Penguin

There is a method to programming that sounds
more abstract than it really is:
Rubber duck programming.

Rubber duck debugging is not a method that is
broken down to the acronym R.U.B.B.E.R
D.U.C.K.

It is a whole lot more simple.
When you cannot get past your current block,
you read your code to your pretend duck!

If you cannot explain your code to an inanimate
object,
then the computer surely will not understand
what you mean.
I do not have a duck
    but I do have a little stress ball penguin.

Keyboard

My keyboard is my weapon of choice.
The way it clacks when I type is actually a
soothing noise
It may get covered in cheeto dust,
but it still maintains all of my trust
My keyboard is one of my favorite toys.

Essoteric

There is a type of programming called essoteric.
It is a form of coding that does not look like you
would expect.

Where normal code looks somewhere in
between machine readable
and human readable-
Essoteric code could look anywhere from
matching the writing prowess of shakespeare to
not looking like anything was written at all.

My favorites are when code is put into the form
of a metal song
and where the writing is done using only the
whitespace of a page.

But if you were following along,
you'd have seen the essoteric language I made
during this particular book.

D.A.D.

I have been reflecting lately on my life and the
jobs I have had

Lots of them paid quite poorly
One of them gave me free pizza and another
paid for college classes
Very few of them were cool with how much I
dink around
Every job had some positive aspect to it

Yet, the best job I have ever had
One that will always be my favorite
Ultimately, was the time I worked with my Dad

9 789357 210904